COMBAT AIRCRAFT

F-15 Eagle

MIKE SPICK

OSPREY PUBLISHING LONDON

Published in 1986 by
Osprey Publishing Ltd
Member Company of the George Philip Group
12–14 Long Acre, London WC2E 9LP

British Library Cataloguing in Publication Data

Spick, Mike
    F-15 Eagle. — (Osprey combat aircraft)
    1. Eagle (Jet fighter plane) — History
    I. Title
    623.74'64   UG1242.F5

ISBN 0-85045-706-8

Typeset by Flair plan Photo-typesetting Ltd.
Printed by Proost International Book Production,
Turnhout, Belgium.

Colour: profiles page 27, © Pilot Press Ltd;
remainder Stephen Seymour, Mike Keep, Brian Knight
© Bedford Editions Ltd.
Cutaway drawing: Michael Badrocke
Diagrams: TIGA
Photographs: Supplied by McDonnell Douglas
Corporation, and the US Department of Defense.

The Author
MIKE SPICK has had a lifelong interest in military
aviation, and is author of several technical books and
articles in aviation magazines covering various aspects
of the subject. One of his leisure pursuits, wargaming
led him to a close study of air warfare, combat aircraft
and the evolution of air combat tactics, on all of which
he has written extensively.

Contents

Chapter 1:
The Eagle Concept   8
Chapter 2:
The Baseline Aircraft   16
Chapter 3:
Missions and Weaponry   30
Chapter 4:
Improving the Breed   36
Chapter 5:
Eagle in Service   43

1
The Eagle Concept

THE McDONNELL Douglas F-15 Eagle is widely considered to be the world's greatest fighter, able to outfly, outmanoeuvre and outshoot anything else in the sky. This happy state of affairs did not come about by chance for fighter design is basically a combination of three factors. These are, firstly, the nature of the threat, either real or predicted; secondly, available technology; and, thirdly, available funding, which is, in turn, affected by the minimum force size considered necessary.

In the second half of the 1960s, the threat consisted of large numbers of cheap, lightweight and highly manoeuvrable Soviet-designed fighters. In distinct contrast, American fighters tended to be very capable, very large and very expensive, the F-4 Phantom II being typical.

Originally ordered as a fleet fighter for the US Navy, it had been developed from an "all-can-do" proposal by McDonnell, a philosophy that served it well when it was adopted by the USAF as a tactical fighter. The Phantom is a weapon system rather than a true fighter and, in Vietnam, was theoretically able to destroy opposing NVAF MiG-17s, MiG-19s and MiG-21s before they ever got within range. In practice, it didn't work out like that, great difficulty being experienced in identification at beyond visual range (BVR) and severe restrictions were thus imposed on the use of BVR weapons, which effectively put the aircraft at a disadvantage.

Below: The high-visibility red paint applied to areas of the wings, tail and air intakes is apparent in this in-flight study of the first F-15A Eagle prototype.

Missile failures also impaired F-4 capability, while the fact that it was not designed for close combat meant that, for a time, it put up a very poor showing in the dogfight arena. Superior tactics, better training and improved weapons went some way towards redressing the balance but the 7:1 kill ratio achieved by the F-86 Sabre over the MiG-15 in Korea never remotely looked like being approached. Thus, by the mid-1960s, it was evident that something better was needed to achieve air superiority, especially if hostilities commenced in Europe, where NATO fighters would be heavily outnumbered by Warsaw Pact aircraft, notably the MiG-21.

An aerial "bogeyman"

Then, in July 1967, the Soviet Union revealed to an astonished Western world what was to become for many years an aerial "bogeyman". A massive twin-engined, twin-finned fighter, the MiG-25 Foxbat showed its mettle just three months later when it broke the 500km and 1,000km closed-circuit speed records previously held by the Lockheed YF-12A, an event which prompted many commentators to reach the conclusion that Foxbat must be better all round, an opinion which appeared to be confirmed by the erudite calculations of certain Western aerospace analysts.

Foxbat was at first perceived to have greater speed, acceleration and range than it in fact possessed, to be fully-stressed for fighter-type manoeuvring and to have an empty weight calculated to be some 25 per cent less than it actually was. Foxbat was mainly an exercise in pushing the limits of Soviet technical expertise as far as they would go and had actually been designed not as an air superiority fighter but a a pure interceptor.

Erroneous reports

Thus, in close combat, the Phantom could have run rings round it but there was no means of knowing that at the time and the general confusion was compounded by reports emanating from the Soviet Union which referred to massive production of the MiG-23, as Foxbat was first thought to be designated. It was only much later that this point was cleared up, the MiG-23 being positively identified as a new variable geometry fighter that had made its public debut at the same time.

Emergence of Foxbat had a considerable impact not only on the F-15 but also on its counterpart and sometime rival, the US Navy's F-14 Tomcat. The US

Below: Sporting a fearsome shark's mouth on the nose and with an eagle motif on the vertical tail, F-15A 71-0282 was the third of ten prototype single-seaters.

Navy's answer was the long-range Phoenix air-to-air missile, whereas the Air Force was anxious to acquire a fighter with a fantastic rate of climb that could reach Foxbat's operational altitude quickly from a standing start, detect it at long range and attack it head-on. Provided that adequate early warning was available, rate of climb sufficient and ceiling high enough, the new fighter would not need to match the Foxbat's tremendous maximum speed. In addition, of course, the threat posed by light, agile fighters could not be ignored, and any new fighter had to be able to oppose these effectively despite being heavily outnumbered.

If this could also be built in to the equation, dogfighting with the Foxbat would pose no insoluble problems as turning capability is essentially a function of speed. Thus, the new fighter would always be capable of outmanoeuvring the Foxbat by virtue of being slower, while, if the Russian fighter slowed down for a turning engagement, it would obviously be outclassed by a fighter that could outmanoeuvre a MiG-21. The best solution to the greater weight of numbers was felt to lie in a marriage of high-technology electronics for detection and weapons guidance with an armoury that comprised four

AIM-7 Sparrow radar-homing missiles, four AIM-9 Sidewinder infra-red homing missiles and, for "close encounters", a 25mm cannon firing caseless ammunition.

Uncertainty over requirements

American fighter development had been on a "back burner" since the service entry of the Phantom, with nobody apparently able to decide what was needed to replace it. The USAF had issued a Request For Proposals (RFP) in December 1965 for a tactical support aircraft, which was not pursued. Then, in August 1967, rather coincidentally just one month after the unveiling of the Foxbat at Domodedovo, a second RFP was issued, this time for a fighter. This resulted in a concept formulation study being awarded to MCAIR and General Dynamics. This was duly completed, and, in September 1968, a further RFP was issued to industry for the FX (fighter experimental), soon to be designated F-15.

At first, a maximum speed of Mach 3 was requested, but, since this requirement was in direct conflict with manoeuvrability needs, it was later dropped. The original eight bidders were short-listed to three and final submissions were made in June 1969. In December of that year, MCAIR was declared the winner, the proposal being for a large,

Below: The two-seat Eagle was originally designated the TF-15A, this being subsequently changed to F-15B. This picture portrays the second of the two prototypes.

twin-engined and twin-finned single-seater. A personal reaction on seeing the first pictures to be released was that it was too close to the Foxbat in general appearance to be entirely comfortable, although a complete departure from the Soviet design was evident in the bubble canopy. In fact, the vague similarity is coincidental, MCAIR and the Mikoyan Bureau having arrived at similar solutions for rather different problems.

Dimensionally, the F-15 is BIG, being rather larger than the Phantom, although weighing quite a bit less. There were two main reasons why it could hardly have been smaller. One was the weapons load required by the air-to-air role. Four Sparrows and four Sidewinders are not particularly heavy, their total weight being about 1¼ tonnes, roughly 10 per cent of the empty weight of the F-15. They do, however, take up a lot of space; the Sparrow is 12ft (3.66m) long and has a span of 40in (102cm) over the control surfaces. Sidewinder is smaller, being 9.35ft (2.85m) long and with a 2.07ft (63cm) span. If the size of the aircraft had been reduced, it would have been difficult to find somewhere to hang them, while their percentage proportionate weight would have increased, with a consequent reduction in performance. The second reason was that the thrust/weight ratio for the new fighter was planned to be higher than anything previously flown, apart from a few experimental rocket-powered types.

A new engine for the FX

The FX specification was intended to produce a twin-engined fighter and the development of advanced augmented turbofans had been initiated for the project as early as 1968. Competition between Pratt & Whitney and General Electric resulted in the selection of P & W's F100 turbofan in 1970. To attain the high thrust needed, turbine inlet temperatures of the order of 1,400degC were required, pushing the technology of the time very hard indeed.

The F100 engine is large and the side-by-side mounting, with separation determined by the demands of the engine systems and accessories and also the main structural frames, dictated the width of the fuselage. Actually, engine separation is very necessary for it aids cooling and reduces the chance of

Below: The large wing, twin fins, fuselage air brake and generous flap area of the F-15 are displayed to advantage in this view of a 36th TFW Eagle touching down.

both engines being taken out by a single hit in combat. Furthermore, in the event of a catastrophic failure in one engine—such as turbine failure or the shedding of compressor blades—there is less likelihood of damage being caused to the good engine.

Where side inlets are used, it also keeps the intake duct as straight as possible and thus minimises flow distortion. This is important, when, as in the F-15, the inlet duct is quite long. The duct itself is normally painted white, for two reasons. In air combat, it is desirable to remain unseen and a white duct minimises the "black hole" effect often presented by a fighter attacking from head-on. Secondly, the white paint should reveal the presence of foreign objects or provide evidence of foreign object damage (FOD), either in the form of blood and feathers, or as scratches.

To return to the engines, these are located at the rear of the fuselage. The previously widely used mid-position caused problems in locating the tail surfaces which is why the rear end of the Phantom looks so peculiar. Previous generations of fighters

needed to have the engines mounted near to the centre of gravity, but advances in aerodynamics and flight control systems enabled them to be located at the rear of the F-15. The nozzles are of a convergent-divergent (con-di) type and are surrounded by a series of moveable flaps, often called "turkey feathers", which reduce base drag.

Unusual air intakes

At the other end, the intakes are of a sharply-raked two-dimensional type, with two moveable ramps to control the air influx and provide a shock-wave at supersonic speeds so as to slow down air being ingested. They have one very interesting feature, the front of the intakes employing variable geometry so that they can "nod" to angles of up to 11deg below or 4deg above the horizontal. Controlled by the air data computer, which also operates the moveable ramps as a function of dynamic pressure, they pivot about their lower edge to adjust the angle of airflow entering the intakes.

In manoeuvring combat, they assist in keeping the intakes pointing into the local airflow at high angles of attack, smoothing it out and helping to prevent

Below: At the heart of the Eagle's superlative performance lies the Pratt & Whitney F100-PW-100 turbofan engine, two examples of which power every F-15 built.

McDONNELL DOUGLAS F-15 EAGLE KEY

1. Radome.
2. Radar flood horn.
3. Pitot head, port and starboard.
4. Avionics bay door.
5. ADF sense aerial.
6. Forward avionics equipment bay.
7. Frameless windscreen panel.
8. Rudder pedals.
9. Instrument display.
10. Head-up display.
11. McDonnell Douglas ACES II ejection seat.
12. Hand hold/step.
13. Cockpit canopy cover.
14. Canopy jettison strut.
15. Tactical electronic warfare system (TEWS) equipment.
16. Canopy actuator.
17. Cockpit air conditioning system.
18. Heat exchanger air exhaust.
19. Intake spill door and hydraulic jack.
20. M61 A-1 20mm six-barrel rotary cannon.
21. Ammunition drum.
22. Upper UHF/IFF aerial.
23. Ammunition feed chute.
24. Starboard wing integral fuel tanks.
25. Fuel vent compartment.
26. ECM antenna.
27. Starboard navigation light.
28. Formation light.
29. Aileron hydraulic actuator.
30. Airbrake.
31. Airbrake hydraulic jack.
32. Flap hydraulic actuator.
33. Starboard aileron.
34. Hydraulically driven emergency generator.
35. High band tuner.
36. Intake duct bleed air supply to heat exchanger.
37. Plain flap.
38. Engine bleed air ducting.

39. Pratt & Whitney F100-PW-100 afterburning turbofan engines.
40. Starboard all-moving tailplane.
41. Starboard fin.
42. Forward facing ECM aerial.
43. Aft facing ECM antenna.
44. Anti-collision light.
45. Starboard rudder.
46. ECM antenna.
47. Afterburner nozzle control jacks.
48. Fore and aft radar warning pod.
49. ECM antenna.
50. Tail navigation light.
51. Port fin.
52. Port rudder.
53. Rudder hydraulically operated rotary actuator.
54. Variable area afterburner nozzle.
55. Tailplane hydraulic actuator.
56. Tailplane pivot bearing.
57. Port all-moving tailplane.
58. Formation lighting strip.
59. Emergency arrester hook.
60. Primary heat exchanger, port and starboard.
61. Port aileron.
62. Fuel jettison.
63. Aileron hydraulic actuator.
64. Formation light.
65. Port navigation light.
66. ECM antenna.
67. Fuel jettison valve.
68. Flap hydraulic actuator.

69. Fuel vent compartment.
70. Outboard wing stores pylon.
71. Westinghouse ECM equipment pod.
72. Port wing integral fuel tanks.
73. Hydraulic accumulators.
74. Engine driven accessory gearbox.
75. Inboard wing stores pylon.
76. Jet fuel starter.
77. Main undercarriage pivot bearing.
78. Forward-retracting main undercarriage.
79. Hydraulic system reservoir.

80. Main undercarriage hydraulic jack.
81. Missile launch rail.
82. Anti-collision light.
83. AIM-9L Sidewinder air-to-air missile (4).
84. In-flight refuelling receptacle.
85. Refuelling receptacle door hydraulic jack.
86. Fire control system missile launch units.

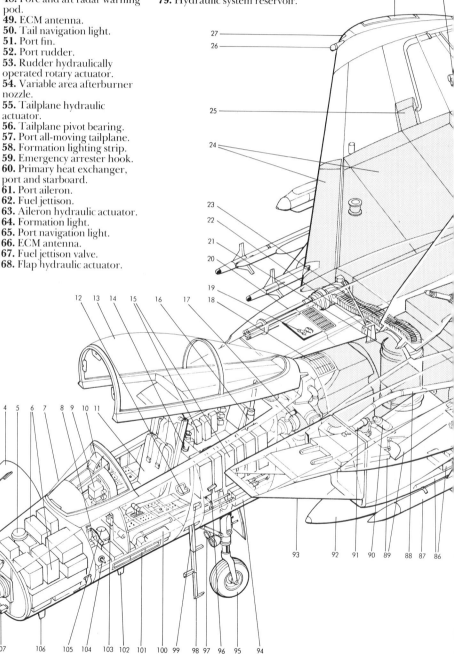

87. AIM-7F Sparrow air-to-air missile.
88. Air system ducting.
89. Variable area intake ramp doors.
90. Ramp hydraulic actuator.
91. Intake incidence control jack.

92. Centreline external fuel tank.
93. Variable incidence "nodding" air intake.

94. Flight control augmentation system equipment.
95. Forward-retracting nosewheel.

96. Canopy emergency release.
97. Landing and taxying lamps.
98. Retractable boarding ladder.
99. Boarding step.
100. Underfloor avionics equipment bay.
101. Formation lighting strip.
102. TACAN aerial.
103. Control column linkage.
104. Incidence probe.
105. Liquid oxygen converter.
106. Lower UHF aerial.
107. ILS glideslope aerial.
108. APG-63 pulse doppler antenna.

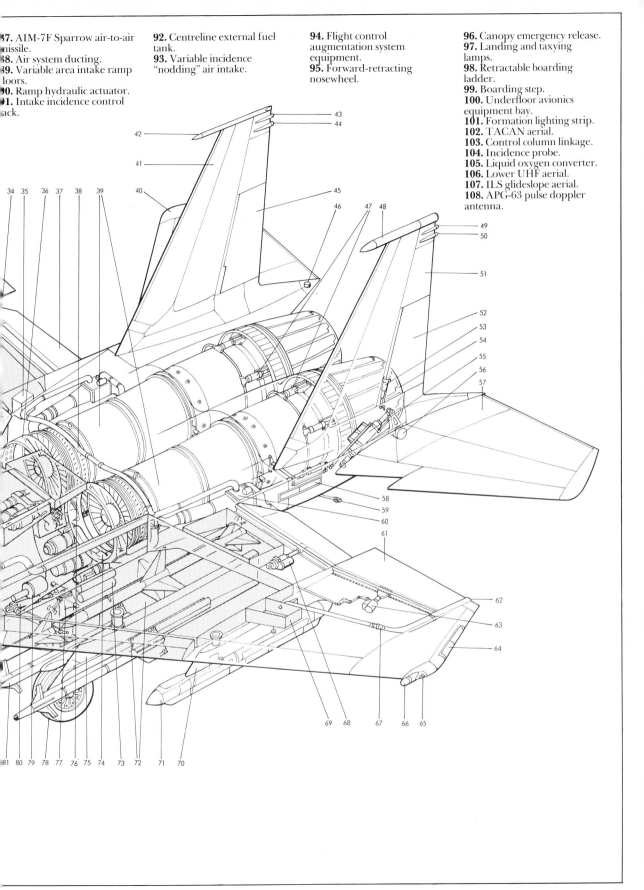

compressor stalls. The previous P&W military engine—the TF30, which is used by the F-111 and the F-14—had been notoriously sensitive to disturbed airflow and MCAIR was obviously anxious to minimise the risk of a repeat performance. On the ground, they automatically nod downwards when the engines are started, ready for the rotation phase of take-off.

It is often not appreciated that the variable intakes have a further function for they give extra manoeuvre control rather in the manner of canard foreplanes. Thus, at supersonic speeds, they help to "unload" the horizontal tailplane, which has allowed this to be made smaller and lighter than would otherwise have been possible. In this respect, they are superior to the strakes which feature so prominently on both the F-16 and F-18 and whose basic function is to create a vortex across the wing.

Appearances are deceptive

The undercarriage looks inadequate for the job, given the sheer bulk of the F-15. The nose gear is long and stalky and looks flimsy, while the main gears are, by contrast, short and have a relatively narrow track. This feature was to contribute to problems at the flight test phase. A tail hook is fitted flush between the engines. On early aircraft, the hook was covered with doors, although this no longer appears to be the case.

The upper surface of the rear and mid-fuselage sections is almost flat, curving slightly around the engine bays as it approaches the rear. In flight, by far

Above: The F-15's novel variable geometry "nodding" air intakes are clearly visible in this close-up view of the nose section, as is the Hughes AN/APG-63 radar antenna.

the larger proportion of lift is generated from the upper surfaces, this plateau-like area contributing greatly to the overall lift of the F-15. Located a short distance behind the cockpit canopy is the single-piece speed brake, this being actuated by a hydraulic ram. It is, quite simply, an awful place to put it, since, when in use, it obscures much of the view astern and, although mainly used on final approach, there is no law that states that F-15s must not be attacked in the landing pattern. However, in designing any fighter, space is always at a premium and it appears that this location was an unavoidable, albeit undesirable, compromise.

The size of front fuselage is dictated by two factors. Firstly, there is the radar antenna, which in turn is sized by the performance requirement. Secondly, it is desirable to achieve the best possible fineness ratio so as to minimise transonic drag. The radar selected was the Hughes APG-63, which has an antenna only slightly smaller than that of the F-14. A direct consequence of this is that the cockpit is distinctly roomy.

One of the most distinctive features of the aircraft is the canopy, which sits high on the forward nacelle, just in front of the intakes, and has a minimum of structural members. The cockpit sills are cut down slightly and the pilot, seated high up on his ejection seat, has an excellent field of view through 360 degrees (except when using the speed brake) and down past the sides of the nose. The windshield is a

Above: Getting airborne in a hurry, MCAIR's two-seat demonstrator, 71-0291, clearly reveals the wide-set vertical tails and exhaust nozzles of the Eagle.

completely curving surface and is in no place optically flat. The canopy is hinged at the rear and is operated by a hydraulic jack.

Low wing loading

In its most basic terms, manoeuvrability in a fighter is a combination of two factors. The first is thrust/weight ratio, in this case conferred by two big turbofans. The second is wing loading, which needs to be low. The wing design chosen for the F-15 is simplicity itself, although, of necessity, it needed to be large in order to spread the loading. It is located in the optimum, shoulder position, which is both easy from a structural point of view and also keeps its members out of the way of avionics and engine bays, thus allowing easy access to these areas.

The wing planform is a cropped delta with slight sweep on the outboard trailing edge.

The leading edge is plain, with no high lift devices, featuring sharp taper on the leading edge and conical camber outboard. Wing sweep is 45deg, the aspect ratio is 3, anhedral is just 1deg, and incidence is zero. The trailing edge contains simple flaps inboard and, rather surprisingly, conventional ailerons outboard. Thickness/chord ratio varies from 5.9 to 3 per cent. The wing area is 608sq ft (56.5sq m), which at fighting weight with 50 per cent fuel, gives a wing loading of 59lb/sq ft (288kg/sq m), by present day standards almost off the bottom of the charts.

The structural elements of the wings consists of three main spars, which are of titanium in the inboard section. In the event of battle damage, this gives a measure of redundancy, as the aircraft will fly, although not fight, with any one of them severed.

One of the few programme failures was the 25mm caseless ammunition cannon. Consequently, the very reliable Vulcan M61 20mm cannon is fitted instead, complete with 940 rounds of ammunition. It is located in the starboard wing root, with the muzzle positioned well behind the intake to prevent ingestion of exhaust gas.

With the engines occupying virtually the entire rear fuselage, the tail surfaces are mounted on short booms outside, and extending astern of, the nozzles. The horizontal stabilizers are set low, away from turbulent wing wake, with a sweep angle matching that of the wing and twin fins are set on top of the booms.

Twin fins for good stability

There are various reasons for having twin fins, although they do as a rule add weight and complexity. At very high Mach numbers for instance, lateral instability becomes an increasing problem and more keel area is needed to counteract it. The fin can be extended in length, at the cost of decreasing its aspect ratio and, with it, much of its effectiveness. Fins are simply vertical wings and aspect ratio therefore has a great deal to do with how well they perform.

With a fighter, high angles of attack may blanket

the fin and rudder and render them ineffective. This is less likely to happen with twin fins positioned on the outside of the fuselage. Alternatives are a very tall fin, as with Tornado, or a folding ventral fin as with the MiG-23. Bearing in mind the wide rear fuselage of the F-15, there was probably not a lot of choice. The fins, with a single rudder, are square tipped and also serve as a housing for various aerials.

This then was pretty much a description of the prototype F-15 (71-0280) as presented to the public on roll-out day, June 26, 1972. As we have now seen, there was a reason for everything in the basic design and the apparent resemblance to the MiG-25 was purely coincidental. In terms of mission capability, the two fighters were poles apart, although this was not known at the time.

Initial contract requirements

The original F-15 contract called for 20 aircraft. These were split into two batches, the first comprising ten single-seat F-15As—numbered 71-0280 to 71-0289—and two twin-seat TF-15A trainers numbered 71-0290 and 71-0291. These were for Category I testing, contractor development, testing and evaluation. The second batch consisted of eight F-15As—72-0113 to 72-0120—and, in contrast to the first batch, which could be considered as prototypes, these were viewed as Full Scale Development (FSD) aircraft for Categories II and III testing. Cat II objectives concerned Air Force development, test and evaluation, while Cat III involved follow-on operational testing and evaluation, the FSD aircraft being as closely matched to the production article as possible.

The first prototype duly made its debut at the McDonnell Douglas facility at Lambert St. Louis International Airport and, unlike many other first prototypes, it had been given virtually no cosmetic treatment, a small McDonnell Douglas company logo being carried on the nose with F-15 logos displayed both there and on the fins, in black.

The forward main gear doors were open while it was on the ground—a feature of all early F-15s—and it was equipped with an instrumented pitot boom on the nose. The only break in the overall colour scheme was the pale yellow, low-voltage formation lighting strips set low on the front fuselage beneath the cockpit and on the rear fuselage just

above and forward of the horizontal stabilizer. A warlike appearance was only evident in the three white-painted dummy Sparrows on the fuselage stations, these being supplemented by an Eros collision avoidance pod in white with a red nose on the front left station.

The roll-out ceremony complete, high visibility orange markings were applied to the pitot, front sides of intakes, leading edges and outboard sections of wings, fins, and stabilizers. It was then unceremoniously dismantled and made its first flight in the hold of a C-5A Galaxy to Edwards AFB in California, where it was reassembled. Minus the dummy Sparrows, it took to the air under its own power on 27 July with MCAIR's chief test pilot, Irving Burrows, at the controls.

Its function was to explore the flight envelope and handling qualities and, later on, the carriage of external stores. It was followed into the air some two months later by the F100 engine test vehicle, 71-0281, and the remaining prototypes followed in rapid succession, the twelfth (71-0289), assigned to tactical electronic warfare, radar and electronics evaluation making its first flight on January 16, 1974. The TF-15As, later to be redesignated F-15Bs, had flown out of numerical sequence, being the eighth and tenth aircraft to take to the air.

External and internal changes

Certain troubles experienced in the early stages of the flight test programme eventually led to external changes, while others needed modifications that took place "under the skin". For example, buffet encountered in certain flight conditions appears to have been due to span-wise airflow. An early attempt at a "fix" tested on 71-0280 was wing fences. These proved unsatisfactory and the remedy adopted was to delete that portion of the wing causing the trouble. About 4sq ft (0.37sq m) was removed from the wing tip, extending back and in from the leading edge to give the distinctive cropped appearance which is still a feature of the aircraft. At a later date, formation lights were added to this raked end.

The tail was discovered to be prone to flutter in some flight regimes and this was cured by extending the mean aerodynamic chord outboard, to give a snagged leading edge.

Both the buffet and the flutter problems were

iscovered and solved at such an early stage in the programme that the "fixes" were put in hand on the production line, prototype No. 3 (71-0282) being the first Eagle to fly with these modifications. The remaining test aircraft were also modified before first flight.

The wing tip formation lights which appear on the FSD aircraft were not fitted to the prototypes. Another difference between the prototypes and the FSD machines is that the former generally had the nose pitot, although this was removable. When not installed, the prototypes featured a small black tip to the radome, this not being apparent on the eight FSD Eagles.

As originally conceived, the speedbrake also caused problems. It was not really large enough and, when fully extended, caused turbulence, with consequent buffetting. The solution to this was to increase its size from 20sq ft (1.86sq m) to 31.5sq ft (2.93sq m) which allowed the same amount of drag to be achieved at a lesser extension angle, thereby reducing turbulence, this modification being introduced by the FSD aircraft. Yet another problem arose during crosswind landings when the narrow track main gear

coupled with the light wing loading caused a distinct tendency to "weathercock", or turn into wind. This

This phenomenon was aggravated by the landing technique adopted. Since no braking parachute was fitted, it was usual to employ a 12deg angle-of-attack and hold the nose up after touchdown, using aerodynamic braking to bring the speed down to 80kt (148km/hr) when the nosewheel would be lowered. However, a crosswind on the front quarter would get under the wing and lift it and, as the controls were then configured, orthodox corrective action only worsened the effect. This was eventually cured by alterations to the systems, assisted by greater nosewheel steering authority.

Excellent handling qualities

Aircraft handling, although pronounced excellent, was initially a little over-sensitive and, to a ham-fisted pilot, still can be, although to a much reduced degree. The control system is duplicated, comprising a conventional hydro-mechanical system, which is generally used as a back-up, and a Control Augmentation System. The system was tinkered with and the result is handling that squadron pilots swear by and not at. Other problems encountered during development concerned engines and avionics.

Below: Evaluation of the variable geometry air intake was long and thorough and included simulated flight at high speed in the supersonic wind tunnel facility at the Arnold Engineering Development Center. Here, a technician checks the intake prior to another test run.

PROTOTYPES AND FUNCTIONS		
Number	**First Flight**	**Function**
71-0280	27 July 1972	Envelope exploration, handling qualities, external stores carriage tests.
71-0281	26 Sept 1972	F100 engine tests.
71-0282	4 Nov 1972	Avionics development, calibrated airspeed tests.
71-0283	13 Jan 1973	Structural test airframe.
71-0284	7 March 1973	Internal gun testing, armament testing, external fuel tank jettison testing.
71-0285	23 May 1973	Avionics testing, flight control evaluation, missile fire control system evaluation.
71-0286	14 June 1973	Armament, fuel and stores testing.
71-0290	7 July 1973	TF-15 two-seater evaluation.
71-0287	25 Aug 1973	Spin recovery, high AOA testing, fuel system and balancing evaluation.
71-0291	18 Oct 1973	Second TF-15 to fly; this aircraft has since undergone innumerable test programmes and featured various colour schemes, including "Strike Eagle", F-15E and Bicentennial paint job.
71-0288	20 Oct 1973	Integrated airframe/engine performance evaluation.
71-0289	16 Jan 1974	Tactical electronic warfare, radar and avionic systems evaluation.

Modern fighter paint schemes tend to be rather dull and, apart from unit markings, are much of a muchness. The prototypes give rather more scope for originality. Most were "air superiority" blue with high-visibility orange trim. Aircraft 71-0283 started out basically blue with bright yellow trim and later assumed the markings of the USAF Flight Dynamics Laboratory Advanced Environmental Control System. This displayed a bald eagle motif on the fin, plus a shark's mouth and eyes on the nose in black, white, and red. The canopy was also outlined in red. F-15A 71-0286 appeared for a while in the air superiority blue which matched absolutely no background in the air and this also had red trim around the canopy while 71-0287 was white with orange trim and differed from the others by having a small square anti-spin parachute box mounted on the rear fuselage above the engines.

71-0289 and 71-0290 are MCAIR's own aircraft and, early in the 1980s, were sporting a gloss white scheme with gloss dark blue trim rather similar to that applied to the early F-18s.

As far as paint schemes went, however, the second F-15B (71-0291) clearly held the prize. Originally finished in air superiority blue, it has been grey, tri-coloured in Bicentennial markings in 1976, when it flew with and without a nose probe while, as the "Strike Eagle", it featured both desert-type browns and "European One" dark greens. More recently, as the Advanced Capability Demonstrator, it has reverted to grey.

THE EAGLE'S RECORDS

Date	Altitude (ft/metres)		Time in seconds	Pilot
16 Jan 75	9,843	(3,000)	27.57	Major Roger Smith
16 Jan 75	19,685	(6,000)	39.33	Major Willard Macfarlane
16 Jan 75	29,528	(9,000)	48.86	Major Willard Macfarlane
16 Jan 75	39,370	(12,000)	59.38	Major Willard Macfarlane
16 Jan 75	49,212	(15,000)	77.02	Major Dave Peterson
19 Jan 75	65,617	(20,000)	122.94	Major Roger Smith
26 Jan 75	82,021	(25,000)	161.02	Major Dave Peterson
1 Feb 75	98,425	(30,000)	207.80	Major Roger Smith

Perhaps the most difficult F-15 for the aspiring modeller to portray is the best known of all, serial number 72-0119, which was the seventh FSD aircraft. This was the famous "Streak Eagle", which, between January 16, and February 1, 1975 set numerous time-to-height records.

"Streak Eagle" was not a standard F-15, but was stripped down to save weight. Among the items deleted were the gun, radar and non-essential avionics, flap and speed brake actuators, one of the two generators, the utility hydraulic system, the tail hook and even, to save just 40lb (18kg) of weight, the paint.

Certain other items of equipment had to be added for the attempt, apart from specialised recording gear. These included an instrumented nose probe, a battery-powered radio and a hold-back device to

Below: Arguably the most attractive colour scheme worn by any Eagle, MCAIR's two-seat demonstrator donned Bicentennial colours for a while in 1976.

llow the engines to be run up to full power on the unway without dragging the tyres around the wheel ims. Only the minimum fuel necessary for each nission was carried and, to preserve balance, "Streak Eagle" had to be ballasted. In all, it was some 2,800lb 1,270kg) lighter than a standard F-15A. The three pilots who took part in the record attempts had to wear full pressure suits and the records they set are shown in the accompanying table.

"Streak Eagle" colouring

The time of year was selected to give optimum conditions for the record attempts, which were made from Grand Forks AFB, North Dakota. The first five records were formerly held by a US Navy F-4B Phantom II and the final three by a modified Foxbat. In all, it was a very satisfying exercise for the Air Force.

Without its paint "Streak Eagle" looks rather odd and the different skin textures are readily apparent; the aluminium, titanium and composite materials contrasting well. The only touches of real colour are the USAF markings and the "Streak Eagle" motif on the nose and fins. It was eventually retired to the USAF Museum at Wright-Patterson AFB, Ohio.

One Eagle that never was belongs to the development phase, this being the navalised F-15N. The Grumman F-14 Tomcat was about 18 months earlier in timing than the F-15 and is a magnificent fleet air defence interceptor and, less generally recognized, a fine close combat fighter. Unfortunately it was also colossally expensive.

Eagles for the Navy?

Seeking a cheaper alternative, in July 1971 the US Secretary of Defense requested the USN to examine the possibility of a navalized Eagle. MCAIR duly produced a modification study which showed a considerable weight increase while a Navy study group also concluded that both weight and cost would rise and that performance would fall to unacceptable levels. Basically, the F-15N would have required stressing for catapult launch and arrested landings. The narrow-track main gear was a distinct disadvantage, while it would also have needed to be made much stronger. The wings would have required high lift devices to reduce approach speed to an acceptable level and the 12deg approach angle would have made deck landing a marginal affair, largely as a result of poor visibility over the nose. The F-15N was dropped, to be resurrected again in March 1973 when the same objections held good. Ultimately, the high attrition rates experienced by American-built aircraft in the Arab-Israeli October War of 1973 convinced the powers that be that no useful purpose would be served by building austere fighters and the idea was finally buried in May 1974.

Below: Rather less appealing, "Streak Eagle" (72-0119) set eight time-to-height records in early 1975 and is now preserved in the USAF Museum at Dayton, Ohio.

2
The Baseline Aircraft

THE EAGLE was designed as an air superiority fighter *par excellence*. We have already seen the measures taken to enable it to outfly any other actual or projected fighter in the world. However, to be able to outfly them is not enough; it also needs to be able to outfight them.

Weaponry is, of course, an important part of this, but the missiles and gun carried by the F-15 are little or no different to those carried by the Phantom during the Vietnam conflict. In future, this will change, but in the early service days of the F-15, this was the case.

Fighter conflict down the years has shown that a small proportion of pilots have scored a disproportionate amount of the total victories. These aces obviously had some special quality that enabled them

not only to survive the deadly arena of air combat but also to be successful even when flying inferior fighters or when heavily outnumbered.

To have an outstanding flying machine and deadly weaponry obviously helps, but, by itself, it is not enough. Pilot quality is a further asset which can be attained by first class training, but even this does not account for the disparity in performance between the ace and the average squadron pilot. Ultimately, no matter how good the average squadron pilot might be and how superior his aircraft, something more was needed, especially in the worst case scenario envisaged, that of an all-out war in Central Europe in

Below: Bearing the markings of all four squadrons of the 405th Tactical Training Wing, four F-15A Eagles enter the approach pattern at Luke AFB, Arizona.

Above: The excellent field of view possessed by the Eagle is clearly conveyed in this picture of an F-15A receiving fuel from a Strategic Air Command KC-135A.

which NATO air forces would be heavily outnumbered.

The quality that distinguishes the ace from the average pilot is a sort of alertness, which makes him difficult to surprise and enables him to use the surprise factor to his own advantage. The recorded history of air combat shows that something like four out of every five victims were either unaware of being under attack or only became aware when it was too late to take effective counter-action. The buzzword is "situational awareness" and the F-15 was designed to allow the pilot to maximise this factor.

In essence, it involved giving the pilot the best possible chance of detecting an opponent, whether target or threat, earlier than he himself could be detected. The pilot thus needed a superior radar and other avionics plus a cockpit layout that demanded the least time spent head down in the "office", coupled with good all-round visibility.

Unlike the F-14, which was considered to need a two-man crew to make the best use of the clever systems, MCAIR felt that they could make everything one-man operable without pushing his work load beyond reasonable limits. Twin-seater fighters have certain advantages, but also some drawbacks. One of the main disadvantages of a two-man crew was the need for them to constantly communicate with each other while, in the Phantom, the use of some weaponry needed concerted action by both crew members which also complicated matters. Thus, the USAF definitely wanted a single-seat fighter to remove these problems.

The most obvious item to improve situational awareness on the F-15 is the bubble canopy, which allows the pilot a field of view extending through 360deg. Clever electronics or no, the pilot still fights looking out of the window unless it is at night or in bad weather. His radar cannot scan astern and, although radar warning devices should inform him of a threat developing from astern, if the threat aircraft is not using radar, but coming on in true

Richthofen style, then the warning kit is of little use, and the pilot's safety is then dependant on his own or, more probably, his wingman's sharp eyes. In a confused multi-bogey dogfight at close quarters, the value of good rear vision cannot be overstated.

The greatest electronic aid to situational awareness is, of course, the radar, which is the Hughes AN/APG-63. This has a maximum detection range of up to 100nm (185km) depending on target size, aspect and reflectivity, and pulse-Doppler modes allow it to look down and detect targets by filtering out unwanted ground returns. Operating in the I/J band, it has a multiplicity of modes which can be selected by the pilot to suit the circumstances. These include search, look-up, look-down, target acquisition and missile guidance, plus a dogfight mode which gives auto-acquisition on targets within 10nm (18.5km), automatically setting a target designator box over the target on the head-up display and thus aiding in visual acquisition.

The greatest difficulty in visual acquisition is knowing exactly where to look and it is in this area that the radar helps the pilot under these circumstances. Target identification is always a problem and an identification friend/foe transponder is an essential part of the kit. A comprehensive electronic warfare system is housed in a compartment behind the cockpit, aerials for this being scattered around the aircraft. Radar warning aerials are mounted in a slim pod at the top of the left fin, while electronic countermeasures antennae are found in an even slimmer pod on the top of the right fin (the prototypes had pods of even size); at the top rear of the right fin, the extreme tip of the boom supporting the left tail surfaces and on the leading edges of both wing tips.

Below: Silhouetted against the setting sun, two Bitburg-based Eagles of the 36th Tactical Fighter Wing perform a routine training mission. Fin-tip ECM/ESM fairings and the "snag" in the horizontal stabiliser can be clearly seen in this fine in-flight study of the F-15.

The radar warning system detects and classifies hostile radar emissions and displays the resulting data in the cockpit. ECM takes the form of deception jamming such as rangegate stealing; noise jamming and chaff dispensing. Infra-red flares are also carried to decoy heat-seeking missiles.

High work load for pilot

The pilot has to fly the aeroplane with stick, rudder pedals and throttles; keep a sharp look-out for other aircraft; navigate; communicate with other aircraft in the formation and ground control and, at the same time, monitor information gathered by the sensors. The work load is high and the cockpit has been designed to reduce it to acceptable levels.

Below: Not exactly representative of the Eagle's usual operating altitude but an interesting picture nevertheless, a pair of 405th TTW F–15s play follow-my-leader along the breathtaking scenery of the Grand Canyon, not far from Luke Air Force Base, Arizona.

Firstly, nothing that the pilot will need in flight is positioned behind the line of his elbows. Secondly, the aircraft has deliberately been made very easy to fly. Thirdly, information presented on the cockpit visual displays is in an alpha-numeric format. This is particularly important in the case of radar, where, previously, raw data which needed interpretation, was displayed.

Naturally, much of the essential information can be transferred to the Head-Up Display (HUD), where it is focussed at infinity, thus enabling the pilot to look at distant objects and yet read the information without having to refocus his eyes. In addition, a new concept—that of "Hands On Throttle And Stick" (HOTAS)—was pioneered for and by the F-15. Pilots normally fly with their left hand on the throttle(s) and their right hand on the stick, and it is obviously a disadvantage in combat to have to use one hand to fumble with various switches, or, even worse, change hands to do so, while trying to keep a

small, distant and rapidly moving target in sight.

The HOTAS solution was to put all the controls and switches generally required in combat on either the throttles or the stick. Things had been moving in this direction for some considerable time, it being a process that had started with the gun button on the stick in World War 1, and HOTAS is merely the logical end product of this trend, with much of the radar functions and weaponry controlled from these two positions, to say nothing of the speed brake.

Manual dexterity an essential

Effective operation naturally calls for a high degree of manual dexterity; one pilot, when asked if he needed to be a concert pianist, replied "no, a virtuoso clarinetist!" Another frequently used item, the communications panel—traditionally sited on one or other of the side consoles—has been located in the front centre top of the instrument panel, where it is in the pilot's peripheral vision as he looks through the HUD. It is flanked by the radar display on the left and the tactical electronic warfare display on the right, to which the same comments apply.

This accent on grouping essential kit around the HUD, although valuable in allowing the pilot to concentrate his vision outside the cockpit, does place rather a premium on his line of sight being forward, and this does to a degree negate the value of the outstanding rear visibility. To offset this, no less than three rear vision mirrors are placed around the canopy bow.

Needles and dials prevail

By the standards of the 1980s, the instrumentation looks rather old fashioned, with a plethora of dials, although it must be admitted that there are not as many as on some previous aircraft such as the F-5E. The combiner glass-type HUD has a narrow field of view by present day standards, but, having said that, it should not be forgotten that, in concept, the F-15 is also quite elderly.

Modern fighters are too complex and too expensive to risk simply showing a pilot the "taps" and then sending him off to fly it. Simulators have great value, but lack the physiological sensations experienced during real flight. Accordingly, it has long been standard practice to build two-seater training ver-

sions of single-seat fighters and the F-15 is no exception.

Originally designated TF-15A, the two-holer has since become the F-15B. The cost of an F-15B is such that it precludes its use solely as a pure trainer and it therefore has full combat capability—in war, it would be flown as a single-seater. In many fighter designs, the extra crew position can only be achieved at the expense of something else. Often a fuel tank has to be sacrificed but the F-15 was produced with the extra cockpit in mind, with a bay just aft of the front seat large enough to house the extra cockpit.

In single-seat variants, this bay represents growth space for the addition of new black boxes as and when they become necessary and, with fighters likely to remain in service for 30 or 40 years, growth capacity is essential. It may also be that, despite the overwhelming accent on a pure air superiority fighter and the slogan "not a pound for air to ground", MCAIR foresaw the possibility of an attack variant for all-weather use which would need to be a two-seater anyway. If this was indeed the case, they kept it mighty quiet at the time.

Below: Dominating the upper cockpit, the F-15 HUD (head-up display) is a vital aid in aerial combat. HUD controls are located on the panel directly below.

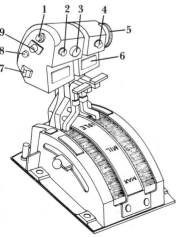

The 'front office' of the F-15 Eagle interceptor is an interesting mixture of old and new technology. Controls sited on the throttle quadrant (left) are as follows: 1: Microphone switch. 2: IFF interrogate button. 3: Target designate control: 4: Gunsight reticle stiffen/reject short-range missile. 5: Radar antenna elevation control. 6: ECM dispenser switch. 7: Weapon selector. 8: Spare. 9: Speed brake control.

Right: The control column also features various switches, these comprising: 1: Trim button. 2: Weapon release button. 3: Radar auto-acquisition switch. 4: Autopilot-nose gear steering release switch. 5: SRM/EO weapon seeker head cage/uncage control. 6: HUD camera and gun trigger.

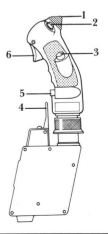

Left: The first two JASDF F-15Js flew from the USA to Gifu in March 1981, final touches like national insignia being applied while in transit at Kadena, Okinawa.

Right: The first fully-fledged JASDF unit to receive the Eagle was No.202 Squadron, No. 5 Wing at Nyutabaru which took delivery of the F-15J in 1982.

Below: The 35th F-15J Eagle to be produced for the JASDF is depicted in the markings of No.203 Squadron, No. 2 Wing at Chitose.

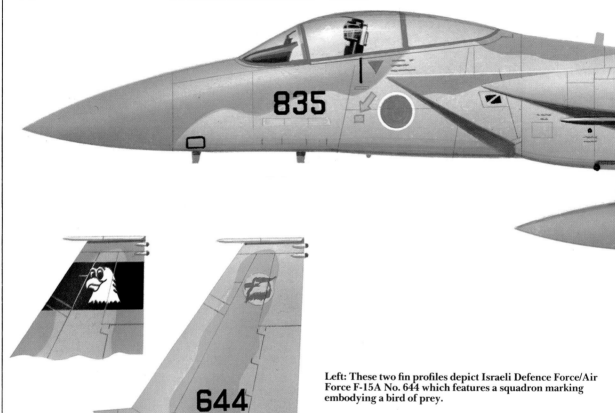

Left: These two fin profiles depict Israeli Defence Force/Air Force F-15A No. 644 which features a squadron marking embodying a bird of prey.

Below: Israeli F-15A No.695 displays novel artwork in the shape of four Syrian roundels, these presumably depicting 'kills', as well as the name 'Skyblazer' in Hebrew characters.

22-8814

42-8835

Above: One of the 15 two-seat F-15Ds purchased for service with the Royal Saudi Air Force, the example portrayed here is from No.13 Squadron which is one of three RSAF units currently operating the Eagle.

Right: In addition to the trainer model, Saudi Arabia also received some 47 F-15Cs like the Sidewinder-armed machine seen here.

ZZ

AF
78 486

Above and below: The 18th Tactical Fighter Wing at Kadena, Okinawa was the first Pacific Air Forces unit to convert to the Eagle, in the process becoming the first Wing to get the much improved F-15C. One of their early aircraft is shown here with a full array of missiles.

The first fully-operational USAF unit to acquire the F-15A Eagle was the 1st TFW at Langley AFB, Virginia.

Resident at Eglin AFB, Florida, the 33rd TFW recently became the first Wing to receive MSIP-standard F-15Cs.

This distinctive marking—depicting an Eagle intercepting a satellite—was applied to the ASAT test machine.

With regard to overseas-based units, the 36th TFW at Bitburg, West Germany, was the first to acquire the F-15.

Above: The camouflage pattern, positioning of US national insignia and the Eagle's distinctive wing and horizontal tail planform may be seen in this plan view of an F-15C from the 18th TFW at Kadena, Okinawa.

Right: Located at Holloman AFB, New Mexico, the 49th TFW was one of the first TAC units to convert to the F-15A.

TUTOR ET ULTOR

Right: Resident at Nellis AFB, Nevada, the 57th Tactical Training Wing is one of TAC's most important units, being tasked with evaluating weapons and tactics.

Below right: TAC's first Eagle unit was the 58th TTW at Luke, Arizona, this later metamorphosing into the 405th TTW.

Above: Initially equipped with the F-15A variant, the Soesterberg-based 32nd Tactical Fighter Squadron now operates F-15Cs like that shown here.

Below: An early production example of the F-15A in the markings initially applied to Eagles of the 58th TTW at Luke AFB.

Above: Wearing the modern fighter pilot's traditional "bone dome" and weighed down by numerous other bits of kit including oxygen connectors, a G-suit and parachute harness, a pilot runs through pre-flight instrument checks before a routine training sortie over a combat range area somewhere in the United States. This kind of scene is enacted daily at Eagle bases around the world, the type now being well established in service in the USA, Europe, the Middle East and the Far East.

Left: The current F-15 Eagle ejector seat is the ACES II type, also fitted to the General Dynamics F-16 Fighting Falcon. Possessing zero-zero capability, it takes just five seconds from initiation of ejection to full parachute deployment.

The only external difference between the F-15A and F-15B is the longer canopy needed to cover the two seats. As far as performance is concerned, the two models are identical for all practical purposes, including combat radius and range. The front cockpits of both are identical, but the rear cockpit instrumentation in the F-15B is austere. All the flight controls are there, as are the radar and the main instruments, including the radar VDU, but there is no tactical electronic warfare display, armament panel, fuel gauge or caution light panel. The HUD is deleted for it would be useless unless the guy in the front seat had a glass head. The side consoles are similarly bleak. The ejection seat originally fitted to both models was the Escapac but this has since been replaced by the ACES II.

Modified exhaust nozzles

Externally, the early model F-15s have seen almost no change from the first production aircraft, but one thing that has occurred on many aircraft is a mod-

eller's nightmare. Trouble was experienced with the augmentor sealing flaps, commonly known as "turkey feathers", and maintenance was time-consuming and costly. The preferred solution was to omit them which resulted in a considerable saving. Base drag increased slightly, but not enough to adversely affect performance, but the exposed lattice of sliding runners and push rods that operate the con-di nozzles looks very complex.

Crew access

Access to all F-15s is usually via a ladder which is part of ground support equipment, but, in emergency or when deployed (the F-15 is self-starting and does not need ground power units), an integral ladder that pulls down from the lower left fuselage beneath the canopy, can be used, in conjunction with an integral recessed hand-hold higher up. This flimsy looking arrangement is unpopular with the crews, who prefer something more substantial.

The final factor built into the F-15 is maintainability. An amazing amount of the skin, some 570sq ft (53sq m) in total, consists of access doors and panels, 85 per cent of which can be reached without recourse to work stands.

Below: In addition to being outstanding in the air, the F-15 is also a boon to maintenance personnel, easy access to component parts for rapid servicing being a keynote of design. Looking a bit like Swiss cheese, this F-15 shows just how many access panels there are.

3
Missions and Weaponry

THE ORIGINAL missions foreseen for the F-15 were threefold. They were: (a) the interception of high-flying supersonic bombers and reconnaissance aircraft; (b) the attainment of local air superiority in the combat area; and (c) the escort of friendly strike formations over enemy territory.

The qualities needed for the high-altitude interception mission are the ability to get off the ground quickly, with a minimum of ground support equipment; a tremendous rate of climb to reach a fast, high-flying attacker before it can pull away out of range; good high-altitude performance and manoeuvrability in order to achieve an attacking position and to prevent the hostile aircraft from escaping; a reasonable radius of action in order to make the intercept as far out from base as possible; and, finally, good detection capability combined with lethal weaponry.

High thrust to weight ratio

The first and last of these factors was built in from the start and weaponry will be examined separately. The tremendous thrust/weight ratio of 1.4 to 1 at combat weight with 50 per cent internal fuel gave the rate of climb that was so well demonstrated by "Streak Eagle". The thrust/weight ratio, combined with low wing loading and a fair amount of body lift, conferred the required high altitude performance; top speed is Mach 2.5 plus, service ceiling 65,000 ft (19,800m); absolute ceiling reached in a zoom climb is 100,000ft (30,480m) although there is little combat capability at this level while the high rate of climb can also be related to the rate of acceleration.

Only in radius of action is the Eagle a bit restricted, the optimum fuel fraction—i.e. internal fuel weight expressed as a fraction of clean take-off weight with full air-to-air weaponry—being generally considered to be about .30. More than this and a structural

weight penalty is incurred, which results in reduced performance. The F-15A and F-15B have a fuel fraction of .28, which was hoped to be offset by the economical F100 turbofans. In practice, it proved to be a little short-legged, a failing that was addressed by later variants. However, endurance could always be increased by carrying three 600 US gal tanks on the centreline and under the wings, to give a further 11,700lb (5,307kg) of fuel, albeit at a cost in performance. In-flight refuelling on the homeward leg was yet another possibility.

Weapons options vary according to model and mission. These drawings illustrate just two of the many alternatives. Below: An F-15E employed in the strike role could carry AGM-88A anti-radar missiles (A); AIM-9 Sidewinders for self-defence (B); the integral 20mm Vulcan M61 gun (C); Pave Tack target designation pod (D); FAST-pack conformal fuel tanks (E); plus "smart" or "dumb" bombs (F) on multiple ejector racks. Bottom: A dedicated air defence F-15 could in future utilize the Hughes AIM-120A AMRAAM missile (C), employing FAST-packs (A) to extend patrol endurance, and the integral Vulcan gun (B).

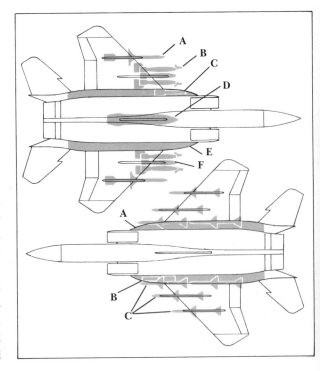

The air superiority mission calls for the ability to detect and shoot at longer range and generally operate at beyond visual distance better than one's opponent. It calls for the engagement of targets lying very high or very low. It requires great manoeuvrability and acceleration once at very close range as well as a weapons system that allows "snap-shots" to be made at targets of opportunity, with the minimum time taken in lining up, selecting and arming the chosen weapon. It needs the ability to sustain damage and still be able to continue the mission. It needs quick refuelling and rearming on the ground, so as to turn around and get back in the air again. Finally, it needs combat endurance, to outlast the enemy in the fight, both in terms of fuel and weaponry.

The F-15 fulfils all those conditions admirably. It has good beyond visual range (BVR) capability with the APG-63 radar and AIM-7F Sparrow missile. This is particularly important in the heavily outnumbered scenario, where it would be important not so much to attempt to destroy an entire hostile formation at long distance but rather to kill one or two to disrupt it, make it feel threatened, and put it on the defensive. Its look-down, shoot-down capability is yet another advantage when defending against a low-level strike in a friendly defensive environment. The low-level attackers would be speed-restricted, almost certainly to high subsonic speeds, while the Eagle would be able to operate at supersonic speed at medium altitude. This speed advantage would enable it to pick its spot from which to attack.

Once visual range is reached, the Eagle's great dogfighting capability comes into its own. AIM-9 Sidewinders will be the preferred weapon here, with the gun available as a close-range "snap-shot" weapon. One school of thought maintains that if the fighter gets within gun range, the pilot has made a tactical error, but, in a heavily outnumbered situation, gun-range fighting will be almost inevitable.

Superior performance and armament

The acceleration and turning capability of the F-15, plus its tremendous rate of climb, will give it the edge over any other fighter currently flying. The final quality, that of outlasting the enemy in the fight, is well served by the carriage of eight missiles, with the gun as a last resort weapon, although endurance could have been better on the F-15A. Close combat calls for the prodigious use of afterburner and this simply gulps fuel. The increasing lethality of modern missiles is making the process of disengagement

Below: Armament available to the Eagle comprises Sparrow and Sidewinder missiles plus the Vulcan cannon. Here, a 48th FIS F-15A lets fly with a Sparrow missile.

from close combat ever more perilous and, if possible, it is better to wait for the opposition to cut and run first.

The escort mission is the most difficult of all. This is because it involves operating over hostile territory, where the advantages of ground radar and control, ground defences, short distance to base and dedicated ECM all lie with the enemy. In this environment, the F-15 is forced to rely almost entirely on its own equipment and resources.

Defending a strike force

The escort mission is no longer simply a matter of flying out in formation with the bombers or strike aircraft and defending them from hostile fighters, if indeed it ever really was. It is a combination of different functions. Thus, a fighter sweep might range up the line of the strike force ahead of it while close escort would most likely involve a flight of fighters following the strike force at the sort of distance at which enemy interceptors would turn in behind to launch their missiles, say four miles (7½km) back. A barrier combat air patrol (BAR-CAP) may be flown to a position between the line of the strike force and the nearest enemy fighter base from which a reaction might be expected.

If circumstances permit, the BARCAP might be set up over friendly territory, ready to interpose itself between the strike force and the defenders. Finally, the escort may take the form of a reception committee that meets the strike force on its way home to dispose of unwanted visitors. Ideally, a combination of all these separate facets would be employed but it is doubtful that there would be enough fighters to go round. Regardless of circumstances, the decisive

Above: Sparrow and Sidewinder missile locations are easily seen in this view of the forward fuselage of the Eagle. The large canopy area is also of note.

factor for F-15 pilots would be the measures built into their fighters to increase their situational awareness, and this would be the Eagle's main advantage, coupled with its exceptional fighting abilities which have already been detailed.

The air-to-air weapons carried are the AIM-7F Sparrow, the AIM-9J Sidewinder in the early days and, more recently, the AIM-9L plus the M61 20mm cannon.

The AIM-7F Sparrow is a semi-active radar homing (SARH) missile, which means that it is guided by

Below: F15 units may be only 15 minutes from the adversary, so such constant training as this 21st TFW machine is undergoing ensures that Eagle pilots would be ready if the wargames had to be played for real.

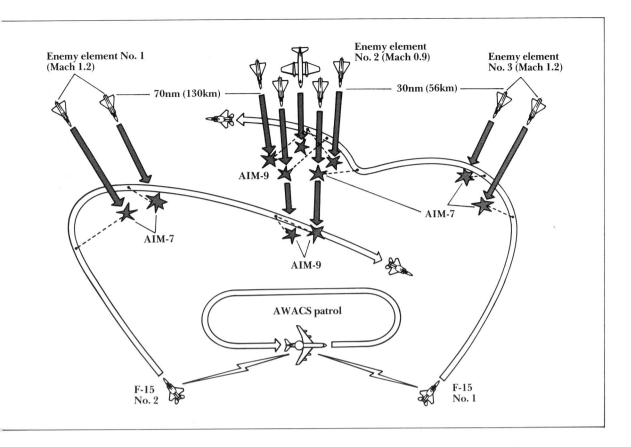

Enemy element No. 1
(Mach 1.2)

Enemy element
No. 2 (Mach 0.9)

Enemy element
No. 3 (Mach 1.2)

70nm (130km)

30nm (56km)

AIM-9

AIM-7

AIM-7

AIM-9

AWACS patrol

F-15
No. 2

F-15
No. 1

Above: Despite being outnumbered nine to two, when working in conjunction with an E-3 Sentry, the F-15 should theoretically emerge victorious by destroying adversaries at long-range with the Sparrow and then using Sidewinder to mop up the remnants. This exercise, conducted on an instrumented range at Yuma, Arizona, resulted in destruction of all nine "targets".

radar emissions reflected by the target. This has the drawback that the launching fighter has to keep the target illuminated during the missile's flight, which makes it predictable for far too long. The AIM-7F is a large missile, being 12ft (3.66m) long with a body diameter of 8in (20.3cm). It weighs some 503lb (228kg) at launch and four are carried conformally on the outside corners of the F-15's lower fuselage. Speed is about Mach 4 at altitude: rather less lower down, and the stated range is 54nm (100km) although in combat this would vary with altitude, target reflectivity, relative speeds and aspects. Effective missile range is always shorter against a target going away than against a closing target, the amount varying with the relative speed of target and fighter. Intrinsically less accurate than an infra-red (IR) homing missile, Sparrow compensates by having a large warhead weighing 88lb (40kg).

Sidewinder is an IR homer and guides on the heat emitted by the target aircraft. Smaller than Sparrow, it is 10.08ft (3.07m) long, has a body diameter of 5in (12.7m) and weighs 172lb (78kg). Maximum speed is Mach 2.5 and range is 9.5nm (17.7km), although the qualifications that apply to Sparrow are relevant for Sidewinder. Essentially a visual distance weapon, the F-15 carries four on wing pylons. The warhead is small, just 22.4lb (10.4kg) and its effectiveness against a large bomber or a tough all-steel aircraft such as Foxbat must be in doubt. The guidance fins on the AIM-9J differ from those of the AIM-9L quite considerably.

Finally, there is the gun. This is a six-barrel Gatling-type cannon with two rates of fire; 4,000 and 6,000 rounds per minute. It is very reliable, but the ammunition could be better for its ballistic qualities are not good.

Weapons for the future

At some future point, the F-15 will be equipped with new missiles. Sparrow will be replaced by the Advanced Medium Range Air-to-Air Missile or AMRAAM. It will use inertial mid-course guidance

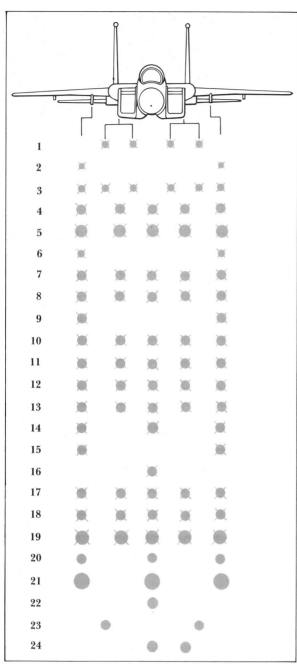

Although the Eagle was conceived as an air combat fighter carrying air-to-air weapons only, successful flight tests with heavy air-to-surface ordnance loads persuaded the USAF to order a multi-role version, the F-15E, capable of carrying a variety of weapons, these being reflected in the drawing above. 1: AIM-7. 2: AIM-9. 3: AIM-120 AMRAAM. 4: Mk82 500lb bombs. 5: Mk83 1,000lb bombs. 6: AGM-65. 7: GBU-8/B or GBU-10A/B "smart" bombs. 8: GBU-12 "smart" bombs. 9: GBU-15 glide bomb. 10: Mk20 Rockeye CBU. 11: CBU-52B/B 770lb CBU. 12: CBU-58B 815lb CBU. 13: CBU-71B 815lb CBU. 14: LAU-3A cluster munitions. 15, 16: JP233 anti-runway weapons. 17: SUU-20B/A bomb/rocket dispensers. 18: BLU-27 750lb fire bomb. 19: Gravity nuclear weapons. 20: 30mm gun pods. 21: 610 US gal fuel tank. 22: AN/ALQ-119(V) ECM pod. 23: LANTIRN targeting (right) and navigation (left) pods. 24: Pave Tack all-weather attack system.

and active radar terminal homing. Unlike Sparrow, it will be a "fire and forget" weapon and, once launched, the F-15 will be able to break away immediately and seek another target.

Sidewinder is also scheduled to be replaced in the fullness of time by the Advanced Short Range Air-to-Air Missile or ASRAAM. It will be faster than Sidewinder, though with about the same range and will fly on body lift, thus having no flight surfaces. It will be compatible with Sidewinder launchers and is expected to use inertial mid-course guidance, with terminal IR homing.

No matter how dedicated a fighter design may be to the destruction of other aircraft in the air, inevitably it will at some stage have air-to-ground weapons hung on it and be expected to perform the attack role. So it was to prove with the F-15. The maximum take-off weight of the F-15A was 56,000lb (25,401kg), while its normal take-off weight in fighter configuration, with eight missiles and internal fuel only, was 41,500lb (18,824kg). This left a healthy margin for carrying extra loads.

The conformal Sparrow stations were of little use for other loads but outboard and inboard wing stations plus the centreline did appear suitable. The outboard wing hardpoints were unable to carry heavy loads and were utilised for ECM pods. The other three hardpoints could be employed for various loads through the use of multiple ejection racks (MERs); those under the wings could carry two Sidewinders each as well as the air-to-ground load which meant that air-to-air armament could remain the same as in the fighter mission.

"Smart" and "dumb" bombs

Each MER was cleared to hold six Mk-82 500lb (227kg) low-drag or "Snakeye" retarded bombs or six Mk-20 "Rockeye" dispensers or four CBU-52B, CBU-58B or CBU-71B dispensers. Alternatively three BLU-27B fire bombs could be carried on each point or a single Mk-84 2,000lb (907kg) low-drag bomb.

Ordnance could also consist of "smart" weapons, a Mk-84 laser, electro-optical or infra-red guided bomb being carried on each point. As all three positions were "plumbed" for fuel tanks, the load depending on mission, could be any combination of these tanks or weapons. The heaviest load is 18

Above: One of eight full-scale development F-15A Eagles drops a laser-guided bomb during trials conducted by the Air Force Flight Test Center from Edwards AFB.

Mk-82 "Snakeyes", weighing, at 560lb (254kg) each, a total of 10,080lb (4,572kg). This, taking into account the weight of the MERs, leaves plenty of margin between the maximum permitted load and the maximum feasible load. Training missions could also be flown with an SUU-20B/A gun pod on each point.

Even with the maximum load, the thrust/weight

Below: MCAIR's Advanced Fighter Capability Demonstrator, 71-0291, totes a particularly heavy weapons load during developmental work leading up to the F-15E model.

ratio remained high and the wing loading low by contemporary standards, the F-15 still being a sprightly performer, although 18 Mk-82s on the three MERs inevitably incurred a considerable drag penalty. It was stated at the time that it could both carry and release multiple stores at supersonic speeds, but the store combinations that this applied to were not divulged. The weapons system was adjusted so that all relevant information could be presented on the HUD and the pilot could thus carry out an attack without having to look inside the cockpit. Weapon selection switches were located near the pilot's left hand, so little movement was needed.

4

Improving the Breed

HAVING successfully developed what is arguably the world's greatest air superiority fighter, the inevitable next step is to try to make it even better. This was the case with the F-15A and F-15B. If the development phase is held back while waiting for new technology to emerge or if good ideas keep emerging and are incorporated into the design as they arise, the end result is a paper aeroplane that never makes the transition into actual hardware. The saying is "the better is the enemy of the good" and the only way to make progress is to freeze the design at a certain stage and then build it. This is not an admission that it could have been better from the start, but, rather, a practical approach to getting an excellent fighter into service when it is needed. Put simply, a good fighter in service today is of far more value than an even better one that is due to enter service in two years time. In all, close to 450 F-15As and F-15Bs were produced at a ratio of roughly six single-seaters to every two-seater before the factory line switched to the next models, the F-15C and F-15D, in 1978.

Apart from improved avionics, the main feature of the F-15C is greater internal fuel capacity. Extra tanks were provided in the forward fuselage, the wing inboard leading edges and behind the main wing tanks, these increasing the internal capacity from 11,635lb (5,277kg) to 13,455lb (6,103kg). A conformal tank was also developed to fit along the fuselage sides beneath the wings to give an extra 9,750lb (4,423kg) of fuel, this comparing well with the three 600-gal external tanks which held 11,700lb (5,307kg) of fuel. The slight shortfall is more than compensated for by the fact that the conformal tanks cause very little extra drag by comparison whilst the three main hard points are now free to carry weapons. These conformal tanks can also be equipped with sensors such as infra-red seekers, ECM equipment, laser designators and reconnaissance cameras. As a result, they are known as Fuel And Sensor Tactical (FAST) packs.

Below: Displaying the code of the 6512th Test Squadron at Edwards AFB, 78-0468 was the first F-15C to be produced by McDonnell Douglas and made its debut in 1978.

The extra internal fuel increases the F-15C's radius of action and combat endurance, while the FAST pack, which can be fitted or removed in just 15 minutes, increases them even more. With FAST packs plus three 600-gal drop tanks, the F-15C/D can make transatlantic flights without recourse to in-flight refuelling. While the FAST pack is described as having marginal impact on the drag factor, it does, of course, add extra weight, which reduces the thrust/weight ratio and increases the wing loading. This, although it has not been officially quantified, must inevitably result in a slight reduction in performance, particularly in the areas of acceleration and rate of climb, although the effect on turn capability should be marginal. The added fuel load led, however, to higher take-off gross weights and potentially higher landing weights, which required a stronger under-carriage as well as better brakes, wheels and tyres. This feature is the only external difference between the F-15A/B and the F-15C/D which are otherwise identical from the outside when conformal fuel tanks are not carried.

Enhanced radar capability

The avionics improvements on the F-15C/D mainly concern the radar. A programmable signal proces-sor has been fitted which considerably expands the capability of the APG-63 by controlling the modes through software rather than circuitry. This permit-ed greater resistance to ECM and, together with a higher capacity computer, allowed for new radar modes. For instance, a raid assessment mode was added which could resolve the mass returns from aircraft flying in very close formation in to individual returns at ranges of up to 40nm (74km), while improved radar symbolism and a track-while-scan mode was also developed. At a later date, a ground mapping mode, with Doppler beam sharpening, was added, using synthetic aperture techniques. Never-theless, the cockpit remained almost identical; the fuel gauges had been expanded to show greater quantities, but little else had changed.

The first aircraft to fly with the conformal fuel tanks had been F-15B 71-0291 on July 27, 1974. The first F-15C, 78-0468, flew on February 27, 1979, followed by the first two-seat F-15D on June 19 of the same year. Even then, nothing stood still for long with the result that Multi-Stage Improvement Prog-

rammes (MSIPs) were announced for all Eagles, Stage I covering the F-15A/B and Stage II the F-15C/D. Both MSIP initiatives involved improving avionic and weapons systems by upgrading the mem-ory system of the APG-63 while also trebling its speed of processing to some 1.4 million operations per second.

Revised cockpit instruments

The armament control panel in the cockpit is to be replaced by a multi-purpose colour VDU, while making it programmable will provide for the car-riage of future weapons such as AMRAAM. All that will then be needed is a software change to accommo-date the new weaponry as and when it becomes available.

In the event, MSIP I was left in abeyance while MSIP II was given the go-ahead in February 1983, the first MSIP II F-15C, serial number 84-001, being rolled out on June 20, 1985. MSIP will eventually allow better radar threat warning systems, improved communications systems and, potentially most signi-ficant of all, provision for the Joint Tactical Informa-tion Distribution System (JTIDS). This system prom-ises a quantum leap in fighter effectiveness, by enabling data to be transmitted automatically and securely between aircraft, the E-3 Sentry AWACS

Below: After equipping the Kadena-based 18th TFW in 1979, European deployment of the improved F-15C model began with the 32nd TFS at Soesterberg, Holland.

and the ground defence environment, thus increasing the pilot's situational awareness many times over. The final change between the F-15A/B and the F-15C/D has been fitment of the ACES II ejection seat, which has supplanted that originally installed.

If the Eagle can be said to have a weak point, it lies in the engine. The F100-PW-100—delivering approximately 15,000lb (6,804kg) of thrust in military power and 25,000lb (11,340kg) using full afterburner augmentation—suffered initially from stall stagnation and was not the most durable of engines. As noted earlier, it was pushing the state of the art pretty hard and both problems have been largely overcome with the result that the F100 is now much more reliable. Nevertheless, the F-15, following the development path of virtually every other fighter in history, has suffered from weight growth and does need extra thrust if it is to recover its former vigour.

Improving the engine

Some idea of the problem can be gained when it is appreciated that the maximum possible gross take-off weight is now a colossal 75,000lb (34,020kg), this having been demonstrated at Edwards AFB in November 1982. P & W has, however, been working on engine improvements and these have led to the F100-PW-220 version. Part of the improvement came from an Air Force-sponsored programme to produce higher thrust, and the F100 EMD (Engine Model Derivative) was tested in a NASA F-15, serial number 71-0287, in the summer of 1983, the results being quite spectacular.

Using military power, at altitudes between 30,000-40,000ft (9,150-12,200m), the EMD-powered F-15 reached Mach 1.15, while it also accelerated from Mach 0.8 to Mach 2 some 41 per cent faster than the standard aircraft. It also demonstrated better durability, carefree handling and superior air start capability. The −220, which has a maximum augmented thrust rating of nearly 28,000lb (12,700kg) will be installed in Eagles from 1986 onwards but no official performance figures are as yet available for this version.

From the time that air-to-ground weapons were first hung on 71-0291, the USAF has shown an ever increasing interest in the attack capabilities of the F-15. The outcome was the F-15AFCD (Advanced Fighter Capability Demonstrator), referred to by MCAIR as Strike Eagle. Later still, it became the F-15DRF (Dual Role Fighter) which, further developed, has been ordered as the F-15E. Due to enter service in 1988, 392 examples of the F-15E are to be purchased. Both the AFCD and the DRF were represented by 71-0291 which was specially adapted for these roles.

Additional air-to-ground weapon carriage was acquired by the development of "tangential carriage" along the corners of the FAST packs, which rendered the Sparrow stations unusable. Offensive capability was to be retained with Sidewinder on the wing pylons and, later, when AMRAAM enters service, this missile will also be carried under the wings. Tangential carriage offers heavy load-carrying ability with a lesser drag penalty than MERs. Maximum

Below: Eagle capability has been further enhanced by the Joint Tactical Information Distribution System (JTIDS), which will greatly boost "pilot awareness" in combat.

oads could be three Mk-83 and three Mk-84 low-drag or "smart" bombs along each side. Tangential carriage can also be utilised by the F-15C/D but this model lacks the night and bad weather penetration capability which will be a feature of the F-15E.

"Missionized" rear cockpit

The greater single difference between the F-15E and earlier models concerns the fact that it is optimised for the strike role, with advanced avionics and a "missionized" rear cockpit for a Weapons System Officer (WSO). Avionics and sensors include the APG-70 radar—a development of the present APG-63—advanced nav/attack systems pre-programmed by inserting a tape cassette containing mission data; Flir, and either a terrain-following or terrain-avoidance system, the choice of which remains open at present. The front cockpit appears to be considerably more modern than that of previous models, with a wide-angle HUD and a moving map display but it is the rear cockpit where the greatest changes are apparent for there are no flight controls. Instead, four VDUs stretch from wall to wall across the top of the instrument panel, all being multi-purpose and managed by two hand controllers. The WSO can monitor aircraft systems, weapon status and enemy defences while using the TSD (Tactical Situation Display) and the SAR display which provides almost photographic quality imagery to assist in detection of targets through smoke, haze or adverse weather.

The F-15E is officially described as being capable

Above: Tangential carriage greatly increases Eagle payload capability. Here, MCAIR's demonstrator gets airborne with four AIM-9s and 22 Rockeye Cluster Bomb Units.

of supplementing the F-111 in the night and adverse weather deep interdiction role. Installation of "Pave Tack" has been considered, this system comprising a pod containing laser spot designators and infra-red trackers, but the final fit is expected to be a LAN-TIRN pod to supplement the SAR radar mode. Weapons fit will depend on the specific mission, but will be more likely to consist of "smart" weapons rather than "iron" bombs, for overflying a heavily defended target these days can only be described as "sporty".

Strike Eagle weapons options

Previous models of the F-15 seldom, if ever, utilise the outboard wing hardpoints, since these are severely weight limited, but the F-15E will almost certainly carry such items as the Westinghouse AN/ALQ-119(V) jamming pod plus possibly a single AMRAAM or the AGM-88A Harm (High-speed Anti-Radiation Missile). Other weapons compatible with the F-15E will include the AGM-84A Harpoon anti-shipping missile and three variants of the AGM-65 Maverick, using infra-red, laser and electro-optical guidance. The French Durandal runway-busting bomb has been checked out and there can be no doubt that tactical nuclear weapons may also be carried.

A close support weapon that can be carried is the

GEPOD 30 gun pod, which can be installed on both inboard wing hardpoints and the centre-line stores station. This is a 30mm four-barrel GE430 cannon, mounted in a pod which contains 350 rounds of depleted uranium-tipped GAU-8 ammunition as developed for the A-10. Rate of fire is 2,400 rounds per minute and the effective range exceeds 7,000ft (2,133m). Lethal against all lightly-armoured vehicles and many tanks, it is also effective against dug-in infantry and its main advantage over stand-off weapons such as Maverick is that it does not need several seconds of level flight while the missile acquires the target, but can be fired immediately after rolling out of a turn. Cheap and effective, it is not vulnerable to countermeasures, but, having said that, it is difficult to envisage a tactical situation where it would be viable to pit a multi-million dollar F-15 against even a mass of relatively low-cost targets such as tanks if they were supported by modern counter-air systems.

Survival requirements

One must have doubts about the efficacy of the F-15E as a supplement to the F-111. It is generally recognised that in order to survive against a modern defensive network and penetrate to the target, transonic speed at ultra-low altitude is needed, with a dedicated terrain-following radar for the night and bad-weather mission. At heights of just 200ft (61m) or even lower, turbulence is severe and the ability of the aeroplane to fly the mission effectively for extended periods—a short time is not too bad but after that crew efficiency suffers—depends on what is known as its gust response, which is basically the way it copes with up and down-draughts.

Poor gust response

Good gust response is achieved by a combination of high wing loading and low aspect ratio, which is why many dedicated attack aircraft, like the F-111, have been designed with variable-sweep wings. The F-15's moderate aspect ratio of 3, combined with what will be, by attack aircraft standards, a comparatively light wing loading, will not bestow a smooth ride at the low levels needed to survive. Indeed, one report has referred to the low level penetration altitude of the F-15E as being 500ft (152m), but this, although it would alleviate the gust problem, is far too high for safety.

The F-15E will be powered by either of two engines. The F100-PW-220 will alternate with General Electric's new F110 of about the same rating. A common engine bay is under development, while,

Above: One new role due to be undertaken by the Eagle is that of "satellite-busting". Here, Vought's ASAT weapon undergoes captive flight trials on an F-15A.

In the future, growth versions of both engines are planned and these should eventually provide augmented thrust ratings of the order of 30,000lb (13,608kg).

The demonstrator for the F-15E programme, 71-0291, has been flown in at least three different colour schemes during the trials period, these comprising air superiority grey, a two-tone sandy desert camouflage and the two-tone dark green livery known as "European One", which is sported by the A-10A Thunderbolt II.

Several other missions have been mooted for the F-15 of which perhaps the most spectacular is the destruction of communications satellites. Dealing with targets in space poses many peculiar problems, not least of which is that, in a vacuum, the blast of an exploding warhead attenuates very quickly, being more or less confined to the immediate area of the gases expanding from the explosion. Shrapnel effect is dependant on enough pieces of sufficient size travelling in the right direction with enough velocity. In the event, it was decided to dispense with a warhead and go for a direct hit.

A contract was duly awarded to the Vought Corporation in 1979 to develop an anti-satellite (ASAT) system. A two-stage missile, the first stage is based on

Boeing's AGM-69 Short-Range Attack Missile, while the second is powered by an Altair III rocket motor. A large missile, it is 17.81ft (5.43m) long and weighs around 2,700lb (1,225kg). Carriage is on the centre-line station of an F-15 which uses a special launch pylon with a back-up battery, a communications link and a microprocessor. Captive flight trials were accomplished in 1983 and the first launch took place on January 21, 1984, at least two F-15s being involved in the trials (76-0086 and 77-0084).

ASAT downs a satellite

Delays in getting an instrumented target into space led to the first "hot" test being made again a scientific satellite on September 15, 1985. The successful destruction of this satellite caused a bit of an uproar at the time, as it was apparently still transmitting data back to earth, despite being near the end of its useful life. While not officially confirmed, it seems probable that a live satellite was needed in order to precisely establish destruction.

ASAT launch obviously needs precision flying of a high order, the F-15 essentially being a third-stage booster for the missile, and it thus has to reach high altitude. Normal procedure will probably entail accelerating to maximum speed, then zoom climbing to 80,000ft (24,400m) when the missile will be launched and it is reasonable to suppose that the position and timing of the F-15 at launch are critical, while the launch angle may well also be.

Another role suggested for the F-15 is that of "Wild Weasel" defence suppression. The development aircraft for this scheme is, once again, 71-0291, which has been fitted out with a chin pod similar to that carried by the F-4G Phantom, this housing the AN/APR-38 radar homing and warning system receivers and antennae. SAM suppression is mainly a job for a two-seat aircraft and adoption of the F-15E as the dual role fighter may well be an influential factor in the possible acquisition of a "Wild Weasel" Eagle (the Weagle?). Weaponry carried in this role would include the AGM-88A Harm, although Shrike and Standard-ARM missiles could also be used.

At present, USAF tactical reconnaissance is carried out by the ageing RF-4C Phantom. A canoe-shaped reconnaissance pod similar to that carried by reconnaissance-dedicated USN Tomcats has been proposed as a conformal fit on the centre-line station of the F-15 but it seems likely that special interface equipment would have to be built in to the Eagle, a few examples of which may eventually be modified.

A STOL derivative

The next generation F-15 may well be a very different looking bird indeed. At present, the Eagle is tied to long stretches of concrete runway, or, at a pinch, motorway. They can get off the ground in a very short distance, but the landing run, with no braking parachute and in the wet, is still considerable. Meanwhile, a new generation of fighters capable of outfighting the Eagle has been planned and this has resulted in a requirement for a STOL (Short Take-off and Landing) and manoeuvring technology demonstrator for which MCAIR has received a contract. The USAF specification stipulates that the STOL Eagle must be able to operate at normal combat weight from a 1,500ft (457m) strip of runway at night, in poor visibility and in a cross-wind in rainy conditions.

The STOL Eagle, which is not scheduled to fly before 1988, will feature two dimensional vectored thrust nozzles, plus thrust-reversing for rapid braking and will also have canard foreplanes with a pronounced dihedral fitted to the sides of the intakes.

Improved performance

The canards and vectored thrust between them should permit flight at very slow speeds, while, by themselves, the canards will unload the horizontal tail surfaces, thus reducing trim drag. The results will be better instantaneous turning performance, greater range and improved acceleration. The vectoring nozzles may also be used to improve turning performance and, at low speeds, will allow the F-15 to "swap ends" very rapidly to offer some head-on discouragement to a pursuer.

A fly-by-wire system will be incorporated which will integrate the functions of the canards, the orthodox control surfaces and the vectoring nozzles, individual operation of which would increase the pilot's workload to unacceptable levels.

Yet another area of development is to upgrade existing sensors to allow the F-15 to make precision approaches and landings without recourse to external aids, which are always liable to suffer battle damage. The improved sensors are intended to make operations autonomous insofar as the recovery phase is concerned.

Finally, the STOL Eagle is to have a new undercarriage able to cope with rough field operation and no-flare landings.

Below: Expected to fly for the first time in about 1988, the STOL Eagle will have canard foreplanes and thrust vectoring to reduce field length requirements.

5
Eagle in Service

ANYONE WHO has seen the Eagle perform a "Viking" departure is unlikely to forget it in a hurry! The rib cage-vibrating noise of two F100s in full' burner; the big fighter accelerating rapidly down the runway, lifting off, then pulling vertically up and still accelerating until out of sight, is an impressive experience. The F-15 is very well liked by the pilots who fly it. As a flying machine it is easy to handle and very forgiving of errors. It is almost impossible to spin; on the rare occasions that spins have occurred, it has usually been due to an out-of-balance condition arising from improper fuel transfer between tanks. It exhibits a certain sensitivity on the controls, particularly in pitch, but this just needs practice to master. The turn capability, acceleration and rate of climb are all much appreciated and I have yet to meet an Eagle driver who wants to fly anything else. On the other hand, the workload caused by the systems is high; HOTAS calls for a great deal of manual dexterity to get the best out of it and plenty of flying time is needed if pilots are to stay sharp.

Early deployment

In the early days of European deployment, Aggressor pilot Capt. Bill Jenkins commented: "Sometimes they are so busy with all the magic in the cockpit that we can sneak up and fly wing on them before they notice." That, however, was many years ago; the F-15 is well established now, its capabilities are well known and its pilots are highly polished performers.

The first operational F-15 was a two-seat trainer, serial number 73-0108, and it was delivered to Luke AFB, Arizona on November 14, 1974. The occasion was marked by a ceremony attended by President Ford and the TF-15A was marked "TAC 1" on the nose. The unit which received it was the 58th Tactical Fighter Training Wing (TFTW) and the first squad-

ron to be equipped with the type was the 555th Tactical Fighter Training Squadron (TFTS), the famous "Triple Nickel" outfit which had ended the Vietnam War as the top scoring unit, claiming 39 MiGs destroyed, 24 of them MiG-21s. The initial colour scheme was air superiority blue but this soon switched to two-tone compass grey. Then in 1977, six Eagles at Nellis AFB in Nevada took part in the joint USAF/USN AIMVAL/ACEVAL (missile and combat) evaluation. Assigned to the 57th Fighter Weapons Wing, they were given a two-tone grey countershading paint job, sometimes erroneously referred to as aspect deception camouflage. There has been some aspect deception paintwork applied to F-15s but this has been little more than a dummy canopy on the underside in matt black with irregular splodges of gloss black to simulate highlights.

Below: Carrying a full array of AIM-7 Sparrow and AIM-9 Sidewinder air-to-air missiles, an F-15A of the 43rd TFS at Elmendorf AFB, Alaska, thrusts skywards.

Countershading—utilising a splinter pattern reminiscent of the Luftwaffe during World War 2—was simply an attempt to render the big fighters rather less visible by darkening areas which would normally be highlighted and lightening other areas. It failed because it assumed that fighters always fly wings level at high noon and in low sun conditions, such as at dawn or sunset, it was actually counterproductive.

The first fully operational unit was, rather appropriately, the 1st TFW at Langley, Virginia, which received its first Eagle in January 1976, the aircraft concerned (74-0083) being named 'Peninsula Patriot'. The first two squadrons of this wing were declared mission-ready by the end of the year, the next unit to equip being the 36th TFW at Bitburg, West Germany. Conversion was, in fact, undertaken at Langley and the first two Eagles—destined for "hands-on" maintenance training—reached Germany on January 5, 1977. From then on, conversion on to the type proceeded apace as more and more aircraft became available.

Eagles at Kadena

The first F-15Cs went to the 18th TFW at Kadena, Okinawa, during 1979, while the new models duly appeared in Europe when the 32nd TFS at Soesterberg in Holland traded in its F-15As and F-15Bs.

Tactical Air Command had had first call on the new fighter, but units dedicated to the air defence of the North American continent eventually began to acquire Eagles in exchange for their antiquated F-106s, a process which began with the 48th Fighter Interceptor Squadron at Langley. Still later, in June 1985, the first Air National Guard unit—Louisiana's 122nd Tactical Fighter Squadron—started to equip with the type. The accompanying box contains what is believed to be a complete list of all USAF units now operating the Eagle.

The Warner-Robins Air Logistics Center (WRALC) at Robins AFB, Georgia also has one F-15 for miscellaneous duties in connection with its function as the primary Eagle rework facility. Originally carrying the unofficial tail code WR—an acronym of Warner-Robins—this aircraft is now coded RG, this signifying Robins, Georgia.

Many nations and services have evaluated the F-15, these including the Canadian Armed Forces, the Luftwaffe and the Royal Air Force. Many with limited budgets rejected it on cost grounds while others, such as the Royal Air Force, needed a highly specialised aircraft for a specialised task. Outside of the United States, only three nations operate the

F-15s SERVING US AIR FORCE UNITS
OPERATIONAL AND TRAINING UNITS

Unit	Squadrons	Base	Notes
1st TFW	27 TFS 71 TFS 94 TFS	Langley, Va.	F-15A from Jan 1976. F-15C from Dec 1981. Tail code FF. 12th AF, TAC.
18th TFW	12 TFS 44 TFS 67 TFS	Kadena, Okinawa	F-15C 1979 onward. Tail code ZZ. 5th AF, PACAF.
21st TFW	43 TFS	Elmendorf, Ak.	F-15A from March 1982. Tail code AK. Alaskan Air Command.
—	32 TFS	Soesterberg, Holland.	F-15A late 1978, F-15C late summer 1980. Tail code CR. USAFE.
33rd TFW	58 TFS 59 TFS 60 TFS	Eglin, Fl.	F-15A early 1979. F-15C/MSIP commenced autumn 1985. Tail code EG. 9th AF, TAC.
36th TFW	22 TFS 53 TFS 525 TFS	Bitburg, W. Germany.	F-15A from Dec 1976. F-15C from Aug 1980. Tail code BT. 17th AF, USAFE.
49th TFW	7 TFS 8 TFS 9 TFS	Holloman, NM	F-15A from Oct 1977. Tail code HO. TAC.
57th FWW	422 TES F-15 FWS	Nellis, Nv.	Tail code WA, formerly 57 FWW/433 FWS. TAC.
405th TTW	426 TFTS 461 TFTS 550 TFTS 555 TFTS	Luke, Az.	Originally 58th TTW, tail code LA. 12th AF, TAC.

AIR DEFENCE (ADTAC) UNITS

Unit	Squadrons	Base	Notes
5th FIS		Minot, ND	F-15A from June 1985.
48th FIS		Langley, Va.	First ADTAC unit with F-15A from August 1981.
57th FIS		Keflavik, Iceland.	ADTAC units do not normally carry tail codes, but the 57th is an exception, employing IS. It was previously the only ADTAC unit with F-4Es and did not carry a tail code on them. First aircraft received late 1985.
318th FIS		McChord, Wa.	
325th TTW	1 TFTS 2 TFTS	Tyndall, Fl.	Tail code TY.

AIR NATIONAL GUARD
122 TFS, Louisiana ANG from June 1985. New Orleans, La.

TEST UNITS

Unit		Base	Notes
6512 TS		Edwards, Ca.	Tail code ED.
4485 TS		Eglin, Fl.	Tail code OT.
3246 TW/TAWC		Eglin, Fl.	Tail code AD.

Eagle, export versions lacking certain sensitive and highly classified equipment in their ECM package.

The first nation to operate the Eagle was Israel, which received its first aircraft on December 10, 1976, under a programme called "Peace Fox". A total of 40 aircraft was delivered quite quickly and two squadrons were equipped with the F-15A and F-15B.

Israeli security gives little away, but it is almost certain that the first Eagle unit was No.133 Squadron. Further aircraft were ordered, but deliveries were delayed as a result of Israel's excursion into the Lebanon. However, latest information states that three aircraft were handed over in May 1985, increasing the total received to 50. Of these, it is known that one F-15B was damaged beyond repair in a mid-air collision with a Skyhawk while on a training mission.

The Japanese Air Self-Defence Force (JASDF) was next to acquire the type, it being redesignated F-15J and the subject of a licence production agreement between McDonnell Douglas and Mitsubishi. The overall requirement is for 190 aircraft and the first Japanese Eagle arrived at Gifu in March 1981, to join the Air Proving Wing. The first operational unit was

JAPANESE AIR SELF-DEFENCE FORCE UNITS

Hikotai (Squadron)	Date formed	Parent unit (Kokudan)	Base
202	December 1982	5	Nyutabaru
203	April 1983	2	Chitose
204	April 1984	7	Hyakuri
207	April 1985	2	Chitose
305	April 1986	7	Hyakuri
301	1987	5	Nyutabaru

Programme name is "Peace Eagle" and normal squadron strength is 18 aircraft.

the Rinji (temporary) F-15 Hikotai at Nyutabaru. This was redesignated as the 202 Hikotai in December 1982 and presently serves as the JASDF conversion unit for the type. A list of present and future JASDF Eagle units is given in the accompanying box.

The Royal Saudi Air Force was next to receive the Eagle, its aircraft being delivered from 1982 onwards and the BAC Lightning squadrons were duly re-equipped with the type. The first Eagle unit in Saudi service is believed to be No.13 Squadron and it is known that it now operates from Dhahran, Khamis

Below: The second overseas customer to buy the Eagle was the JASDF which requires about 190 aircraft, most of which will be built under licence by Mitsubishi.

Mushayt and Taif. Some 62 aircraft were procured under the "Peace Sun" programme, this figure including two F-15C attrition reserves initially held in the USA. At least one Saudi aircraft has been lost in a landing accident and further procurement appears to have been ruled out by the recent large order for the Tornado and by the "Camp David" peace agreement which stipulated that no more than 60 F-15s may be based in Saudi Arabia.

The combat capability of the F-15 was extensively tested in the United States in the mid-1970s. Aircraft from Eglin AFB successfully intercepted drones flying at Mach 2.7 at 70,000ft (21,300m) while, later, over the Navy test range at China Lake, California, a succession of one versus one combats were simulated against different types, the results being outstanding.

Victories were recorded in four combats against the A-37, 46 engagements with the T-38, simulating the MiG-21, 29 engagements against F-5Es also simulating the MiG-21, 17 engagements against the A-4 simulating the MiG-17, 13 engagements against the F-106 simulating the MiG-23 and no less than 67 engagements against the Phantom, also simulating the MiG-23. There were just two ties—both against the Phantom—where neither aircraft "fired".

The acceleration and turning capability combined with the superb weapons system to make the F-15 a world-beater. It is stressed to take plus 9g and minus 3g loadings, which is a great asset in combat, but sometimes not so good in training. In one practice combat in the early-1980s, an Eagle driver launched himself from 20,000ft (6,100m) at a target aircraft at 13,000ft (3,950m). At an airspeed of 500kts (927km/hr), he let his nose get too low and commenced a hard pull-up, reaching 9g and recovering to level flight at 5,000ft (1,500m). Inevitably, his head was forced down against his chest and he ended the flight with a compression fracture of the seventh vertebra in his neck. Clear evidence that there are times when the sparkling performance of the Eagle must be treated with care.

Combat action

The Eagle has also seen combat action with two air forces, namely those of Israel and Saudi Arabia. Of the two, the Israeli machines have seen by far the bulk of the action.

Blooding of the Eagle came on June 27, 1979 when a mixed force of F-15s and Kfirs covered a strike force attacking terrorist bases in Southern Lebanon. Between eight and a dozen Syrian MiG-21s tried to intervene, were detected by a supporting Israeli Hawkeye and were thoroughly bounced by the escorts, losing five of their number; four of them falling victim to Eagles. Intermittent clashes occurred subsequently and the Eagle score gradually built up.

Below: As far as combat is concerned, Israel's Defence Force/Air Force leads the way, IDF/AF F-15s having already accounted for more than 50 assorted MiGs.

ISRAELI EAGLE KILLS

Type	Total	Weapons used where known
MiG-21	15½*	6 with Sparrow 4½ with Sidewinder or Shafrir 2 with cannon fire 5 unknown (*denotes 2 probables)
MiG-23	3	Unknown
MiG-25	3	All Sparrow.
"MiGs"	34	Unknown. Believed to be mainly MiG-23s and Su-22s, but possibly included some Su-17s.
Helicopters	1	Probably cannon fire

Then, on March 13, 1981, a "Foxbat" tried to intercept an Israeli RF-4E and was downed by a Sparrow fired from an escorting F-15. The Eagle had at last triumphed over the aircraft which it had been designed to match.

The next Eagle victim was yet another "Foxbat", hit by a Sparrow on July 29, 1981, again while trying to intercept an RF-4E. Meanwhile, the F-16 strike on the Iraqi nuclear reactor near Baghdad had been flown the previous month and, while the F-16 was rightly given the credit for bombing this target, F-15s provided the fighter escort.

On June 6, 1982, Israel launched the "Peace for Galilee" operation, namely the invasion of Southern Lebanon. Over the next few days, a series of massive dogfights took place above the Bekaa Valley as the Syrian Air Force attempted to assert itself. The result was, quite literally, a disaster for them; over 80 aircraft being lost in air combat at no cost to the Israelis. As would be expected, the F-15 performed excellently, accounting for no fewer than 42 Syrian aircraft. Full details of Eagle victories in Israeli service are not available, but the table details data that had been made available to August 31, 1982, when yet another "Foxbat" fell to an Eagle.

The record of the F-15 in Israeli service—with a kill/loss ratio of 56.5 to zero—has never been surpassed in the history of air combat, but, even then, it was not all over. On October 1, 1985, the Israeli Air Force mounted a long-range strike against PLO headquarters in Tunisia. Originally thought to have been carried out by F-16s escorted by F-15s, it is now believed that only the F-15 was involved. The raid involved a round-trip of roughly 2,600nm (4,800km), carrying 1,000lb (454kg) iron bombs, as well as some laser-guided weapons. Three in-flight refuellings were needed and support was also given by ECM aircraft.

The final air combat victories to date have, ironically enough, been scored against earlier fighters produced by McDonnell Douglas. On June 5, 1984, a USAF E-3 AWACS on patrol over the Persian Gulf detected two Iranian fighters approaching Saudi Arabian airspace. Two Saudi Eagles were vectored to the scene and launched Sparrows at the intruders, which proved to be F-4E Phantoms. Both were knocked down.

Below: Caught just before landing, F-15A No.672 typifies Israeli Eagles with regard to presentation of national markings. As usual, unit insignia has been censored.

Above: Some idea of the multitude of weapons options available to the Eagle can be gained from close study of this picture of a **TF-15A test specimen at Edwards AFB in the early '70s. New weapons and other stores can now be added to the display.**

F-15 EAGLE WEIGHTS

Figures given are lb(kg) and are approximate

	F-15A	F-15B	F-15C	F-15D	F-15C with FAST pack
Empty	28,000 (12,700)	28,600 (12,973)	29,180 (13,236)	29,780 (13,508)	30,300 (13,699)
Takeoff in fighter configuration, intl fuel, 8 missiles	41,500 (18,824)	42,300 (19,187)	44,500 (20,185)	45,300 (20,548)	55,270 (25,070)
Max TOGW	56,500 (25,401)	56,500 (25,401)	68,000 (30,844)	68,000 (30,844)	68,000 (30,844)
Combat wt, 8 missiles and 50% intl fuel	35,680 (16,184)	36,280 (16,457)	37,772 (17,133)	38,573 (17,496)	43,668 (19,808)
Internal Fuel	11,635 (5,277)	11,635 (5,277)	13,455 (6,103)	13,455 (6,103)	23,205 (10,526)
Fuel in FAST packs	N/A	N/A	9,750 (4,423)	9,750 (4,423)	N/A
Fuel carried externally in three 600 US gal tanks	11,700 (5,307)	11,700 (5,307)	11,700 (5,307)	11,700 (5,307)	11,700 (5,307)
Max weapon load	12,000 (5,543)	12,000 (5,543)	16,000 (7,258)	or 18,000 (8,165)	with tangential carr.

LOADINGS (all at combat weight)

	F-15A	F-15B	F-15C	F-15D	F-15C with FAST pack
Wing loading (lb/ft^2-kg/m^2)	59 (288)	60 (293)	62 (303)	63 (308)	72 (351)
Thrust loading (lb/lb kg/kg)	1.40 (0.63)	1.38 (0.62)	1.32 (0.60)	1.30 (0.59)	1.15 (0.52)

Note: Little data is available on the F-15E except that a max TOGW of 81,000lb (36,742kg) is proposed.

DIMENSIONS,

All models (A, B, C, D, & E) identical

Length	63.75ft (19.43m)
Wing span	42.81ft (13.05m)
Fin height	18.46ft (5.63m)
Tail span	28.25ft (8.61m)
Main gear track	9.03ft (2.75m)
Wing area	608ft^2 (56.5m^2)

ENGINE DETAILS

Type	Pratt & Whitney F100-PW-100
Military thrust	16,200lbs (7,348kg)
Augmented thrust	25,000lbs (11,340kg)
Military sfc	0.68lbs/lb(0.31kg/kg)
Augmented sfc	2.55lbs/lb (1.16kg/kg)
Length	15.92ft (4.85m)
Diameter	4.25ft (1.30m)
Weight	2,855lbs (1.295kg)

PERFORMANCE

V max at altitude	Mach 2.5+
V max at sea level	Mach 1.2
Initial climb rate	50,000 ft/min (254m/sec)
Minimum control speed	100kt (185km/hr)
Unrefuelled duration	5.25 hour (with conformal tanks)
Refuelled duration	14.25 hours
Service ceiling	65,000ft (19,800m)
Absolute ceiling	100,000ft (30,480m)
Design loadings	+9g/−3g
Instantaneous turn	14.1 degrees/sec
Sustained turn	11.8 degrees per second

PRINTED IN BELGIUM BY proost INTERNATIONAL BOOK PRODUCTION